CONTENTS

Introduction
by Professor Martin Attrill
Director, Marine Institute
Plymouth University

Poems

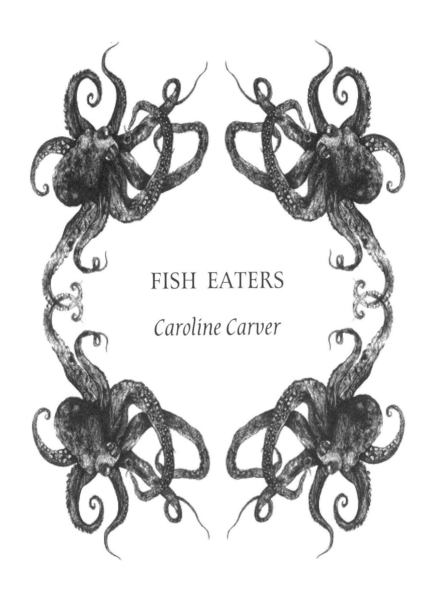

FISH EATERS

Caroline Carver

First published in the United Kingdom in 2015 by

University of Plymouth Press, Drake Circus, Plymouth, Devon, PL4 8AA, United Kingdom

Paperback ISBN 978-1-84102-397-7
Hardback ISBN 978-1-84102-398-4

© University of Plymouth Press 2015

The rights of Caroline Carver as author and Thomas Barwick, Sam Marsh, Ben Wills, Becca Collins, Lizzie Foster-Turner, illustrators and Justin Spray, Lloyd Russell and Alan Stewart, photographers and Dr Richard Kirby as photographic illustrator, have been asserted by them in accordance with the Copyright, Designs and Patents Acts 1998

A CIP catalogue record of this book is available from the British Library

Publisher: Paul Honeywill

Concept: Tim Guy

Design: Matthew Grocutt

Typeface: Emilida, commissioned by Tim Guy as part of the EMI Group corporate identity by Lida Cardozo Kindersley and digitised by Eiichi Kono

Paper: Antalis (UK) Explorer uncoated stock, cover 300 gsm, text 190 gsm

Editor: Dr Alyson Hallett

Proof reader: Michael Carver

Print preparation: Toucan Design, Exeter

Illustrations

Thomas Barwick
Cover, buoys 2-3, wave 6, buoys 8-9, wave & buoy 8-9, wave 10-11, waves 24-25, seahorses 28-29, wave 32-33, buoy 41
tom.barwick@plymouth.ac.uk

Sam Marsh
eels 3, jellyfish 17

Ben Wills
Octopi 1, octopi 7, 'Ancestor' fish 10, waves 26
ben.willsart@gmail.com

Becca Collins
island 36
beccacollinsillustration@gmail.com

Lizzie Foster-Turner
boat 30, seascape 34, boat and moon 40
lizziefosterturner@gmail.com

Photography

Justin Spray, Photographer, inside front and back covers 12, 14-15, 39
justinspray@mendas.com

Dr Richard Kirby, photographic illustration, 20, 22
richard.kirby@planktonpundit.org

Lloyd Russell, Photographer, 4
lloyd.russell@plymouth.ac.uk

Alan Stewart, Photographer, 5
alan.stewart@plymouth.ac.uk

Printed and bound by Short Run Press Exeter, EX2 7LW, United Kingdom

for Martin Attrill and Tim Guy
who sent me on wonderful voyages

and for Daria
who swims like a fish

the stone appears to have stepped further away from the building -
like a woman being dressed in her wedding finery

she's moved into her own large house
high-ceilinged   roomy   full of new light

where her designer weaves spells
and two men kneel at her feet

adding last touches to the bottom of her skirt
it doesn't matter that the room's built of plywood
with a plastic corrugated roof

it's been transformed
for this day only
into something like a film set

the cameraman fits himself onto the scaffolding
a Tarzan of the pipes
(in a way that would make health and safety blench)

he's having fun   among his metal branches
and the director's smiling
the stone-cutter's smiling
the men at her feet are the only ones not smiling

a stream of concentration flows through their arms
and onto the stone
as they complete their difficult task

and the stone herself?
she's silent   serene   Madonna-like
smiling her secrets to herself
waiting for her Very Big Day

Introduction

A building brought Caroline and me together. Our Plymouth University Marine Building, opened in 2012, enabled us to design a bespoke interdisciplinary space and from the start one objective was to bring together science, engineering and arts as part of the internal design. Together with graphic artists and underwater photographers, Caroline produced a series of poems inspired by the building, the work that was to be undertaken within it, and the people who would inhabit it. The result was a series of lines and snippets from Caroline's work that form part of the fabric of the building and create a poem of each person's making as they journey through the building. I regularly give tours of our amazing new facilities, such as wave tanks and ship simulators, to visiting dignitaries and interested parties, and regularly they stop and read Caroline's words which complement and extend the experience of the building and its facilities.

It was clear that such a unique collaboration couldn't stop there, so we were proud to make Caroline one of five Artists in Residence at the Marine Institute, complementing the writer, composer, video and performance artists who take their inspiration from the marine environment, and our staff engaged with exploring it. Through her work, Caroline engaged with a range of science and engineering research groups, finding out about their work and their passion and excitement for what they do and for the marine realm generally, spinning out from this to connect with local schools and academies. Their words inspired her words. She also gave much back, hosting lunchtime poetry writing sessions for staff who found this a valuable form of meditation, relaxation, enabling them to express their deeper thoughts and feelings about what they do and the ocean in which they work. *Fish Eaters* demonstrates the depth and breadth of Caroline's journey through the multifaceted marine expertise, facilities and ideas that the Marine Institute represents, capturing flashes of visions and concepts and reimaging them into something new, unexpected and beautiful; sometimes still recognisable, sometimes an unimagined creation. And with "at sea with poetry" it all returns once again to that start point: the building itself.

Often people wonder about the diversity and feasibility of something like the Marine Institute: how can people working in engineering, science, navigation, law, art, psychology, business, computing, conservation, music possibly be linked? But the ocean has a draw and a power that I feel no other part of our earth has. It's deep-rooted, spiritual, it captures people from an early age and then doesn't let go, and so we find disparate and sometimes convoluted ways of staying connected, to be able to say "we work on the sea". *Fish Eaters* expresses all that perfectly.

Professor Martin Attrill
Director, Marine Institute
Plymouth Univerity

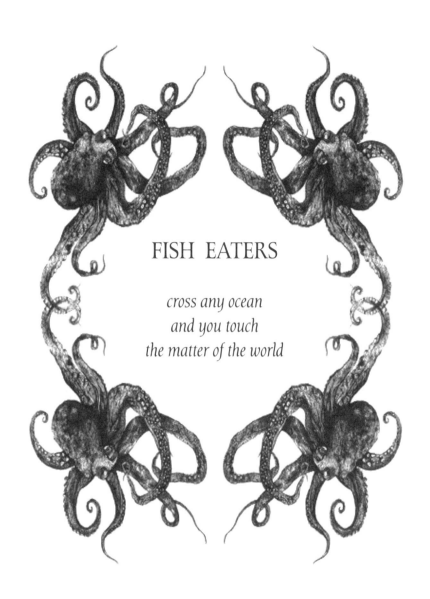

FISH EATERS

*cross any ocean
and you touch
the matter of the world*

blue whale

when he lived on land
instead of under the sea
he dreamed apple blossom mixed with honey

    his living space was hung
    with all the colours of the orient

        residual legs faded
        with each step
        up the evolutionary ladder

why tell him he's as long as a football pitch?
his 'fields' reach skywards

        in the last battle
        harpoons will be the weapon of choice

all the king's men jump onto their horses
bending over their necks   their long whale backbones

no   all the king's men jump into their boats
flensing knives waiting
on the ships behind them

        the sound of his voice fades from five oceans

        his eye is a one-way mirror

once this was a kingdom without whales
beaches were empty of them
the lamps of the world had no oil

when he lies on the surface
in the arms of Morpheus
what dreams fill
the half of his mind that's asleep?

(humbacks
sleep like caryatids
upright as pillars of Solomon)

I was a midwife
when her calf was born
pulled this new world   tail-first   out of her

the head   last   nudged upwards
for its first breath

she jetted her milk out generously
enough for a small herd of cows

soon I will become a sea serpent
I want to be large enough
to clasp her baby in my arms

when you went back
why did you keep your land-borne lungs
the wombs of your females
your milky calves?

why do you drink fresh water
flavoured by sea?   swelling and pleating your throat
to filter cornucopias of krill

there's no longer room for you
in our world
you take too much space

I lie on the seabed
whales like ocean-going ships
pass above me

one day he'll teach me
how to breathe again

dreaming the ancestor

something's climbing out of the sea
legs barely able to support its heavy body

later it will go back   become a whale

but my dream always takes me further up the family tree
fogged by shifting clouds
aeons   light years
till I come to a creature
deciphered from archeological fragments
four-legged   shapeless   inert

and it's lying on its side like a dog that's run too many miles
and it's lying on its side as if weary of the idea of becoming human
and it's lying on its side beacuse it wants to turn round and go back

le déluge

land's turning back to sea again   homes to Noah's arks
in preparation for the floods already with us

in our new-built ocean-going vessel of a house
we debate which creatures to include   how many
the mind boggling at what below-decks life
must have been like that other time
the noise the general overcrowding
the urge to leave out stoats magpies moles
some of the slimier creeping things

I've looked at pictures of 3-metre squid
resolving never to dive deep enough to find them
maybe we could leave out giant jellyfish
gulls that prey on fledglings diving from cliffs
or baby turtles scurrying for their first taste of sea
come to that   do we ban killer whales
who snap up penguins   so solemn
in their good parenting
so stoic in the great antarctic winds?

and how will polar bears get on with seals
in the great ocean aquarium we have to fit on board
to hold the plankton?...

                    ... hold on missus
                    what the point this crazy poem?

                    it the ocean   man
                    it the ocean we gotta keep safe

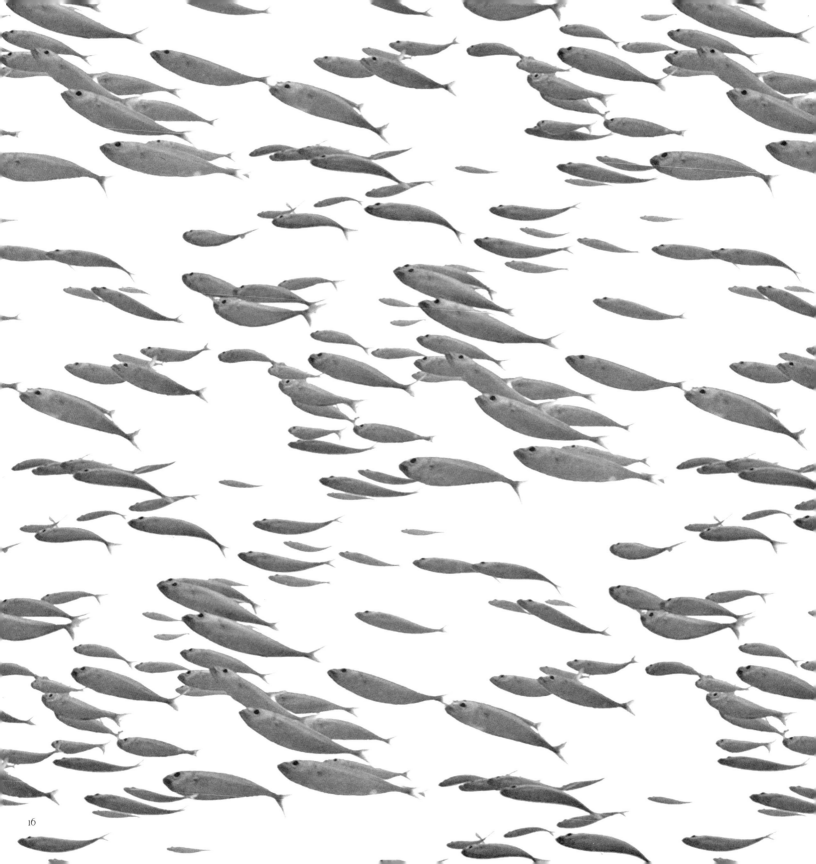

Gaia uncertain

she talks to fishes   scoops them up
in petulant moues of colour   they watch
open-mouthed as she gathers her skirts
fills the sky with rainbows

drown them they say mimicking human-
speak   she prefers it when they use
their own language
simple   without rancour

today they're as upset as she is
swimming in ever tighter circles
light the volcanoes they say burn forests
send tsunami   viruses   drought   famine   flood

Gaia listens carefully
and what's a girl to do if she cares about
herself ?   she smiles
at her reflection in the moon mirror
wraps jet-streams round her throat
like wintry scarves

17

Aquarius

for Penny

drifting across great stretches of ocean
like the hippie you were   in time long gone
you suddenly sit up in your boat or your bed
or wherever you've chosen to be dreaming this day
because your muse is murmuring in your ear
you're   disconnected   disconnected   disconnected
something   he goes on   is not sitting right with you
and he's damn right nothing anywhere is sitting right
and one of the things about being at sea is
there are no boundaries   not a fence in sight
the only things sitting right
now you mention sitting right as important
are things not held by gravity
but displacement of water   the ones
that defy geometry   move godlike up and down
all planes of depth and shadow   shift
in and out of minds   even of those
who've never seen them   as they make their way
in the world of Aquarius

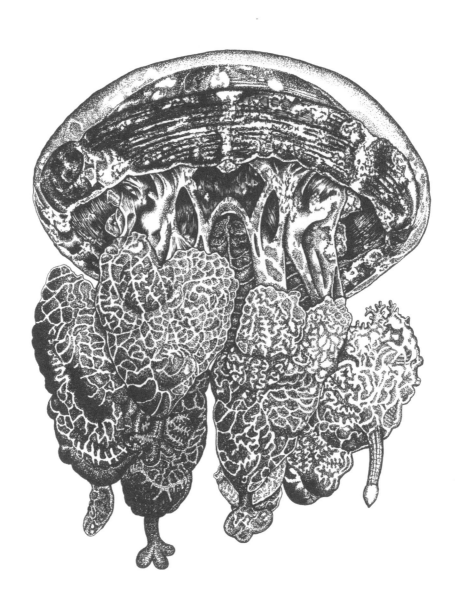

nightsweats *filling my bed*
with an ocean created out of my own body

the reminder I can't touch even a lover's hand
because so many layers of water lie between us

people pluck seaweed from the fields
if I lick my fingers   they taste of salt

libation

in this bottle I bring whale water   filled
with mind-boggling quantities of krill
to keep the largest mammal in the world
            moving   singing   sleeping
birthing babies the size of elephants

in this bottle I bring air   rank
with halitosis   pressure-hosed
to the surface by a marine creature
            which can't breathe underwater -
unwrap the bottle carefully

prise petroleum-sourced bubble-wrap
apart from its tape bandages
            un-stop the phial   made from fire
and pulverised grains of sand
empty it carefully over your feet

there's always danger
there may be a genie in the bottle
who will blow you away   pfffffffff
            like a yacht scudding over the waves
in front of one of those jaunty puff-

cheeked trade winds you find on old maps

till you're beached   high and dry
head over tail   arse over tit
            washed up
stranded . . .

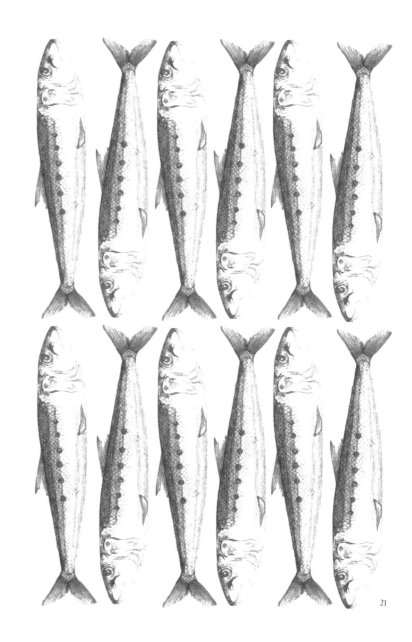

21

sleeping giants

blue whales don't breathe
by instinct   can't have that
gosh I went right out   or
wait till I tell you
what I dreamed about last night   baby
kind of sleep
always
they must keep
half their brains awake
reminding them when
to come up for air

unlike dogs
chasing rabbits in their dreams
whales lie passively
near the sea surface
while their bodies refuel
restore hormone balances
stabilise memory
                              probably
never revisit   in technicolour
or even black and white
those glorious   gourmand-y
glutinous banquets of krill

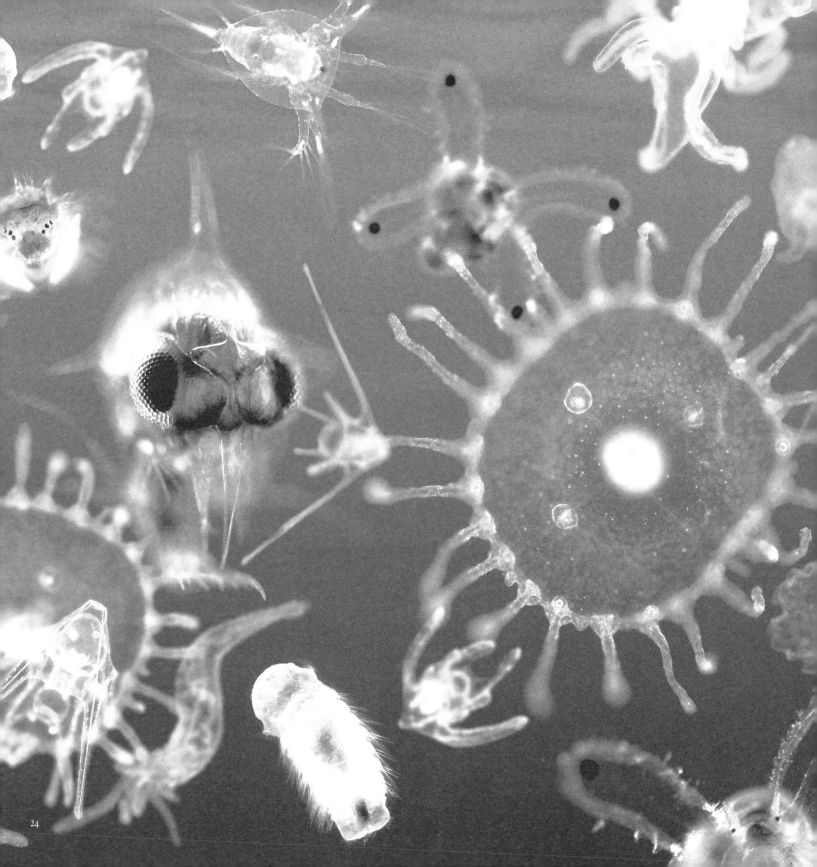

plankton

Atlas may support the world
on his two strong arms
but creatures smaller
than the thinnest strands of hair
are harnessing sunlight
creating
more than half the air we breathe
rain   clouds
the invigorating smell of sea

their tiny mirrors   visible from space
sparkle as if the world's turned upside down

and the sea's full of stars

legend has it
their bloom of foam
gave birth to Aphrodite
the most beautiful woman in the world

ocean silk roads

like fishermen of the moon
laboratory technicians
have installed this drum
with its layers of finest Shanghai silk
which now stream out behind our ferry
collect samples of plankton
'precious as rubies'
before winding them in for their last journey
back to the lab   perhaps
                    no worse an end
than any other

counting the infinite

today the sea is blue deep blue
showing what is there and what is not there
as if colour's falling from the sky
like water returning to itself
made blue or brown or green or even white
by tiny phytoplankton floating near the surface
communing with the sun

armed with only a tape measure
and a wooden disk
citizen scientists
like doctors
with stethoscopes
lean over the sides of their boats
watching this small circle
drift down through blue
or brown or green or white
until it fades from sight
so they can gauge the health of our oceans
beam their findings
up to the watching satellite

at sea with poetry
The Marine Institute, Plymouth University, UK

water breathes energy into all the spaces
of this building   making waves of phenomenal exactitude
or sleeping with a profound stillness

banks of sophisticated equipment
test beach erosion hull behaviour
tidal surge   storms   and the effects of tsunami

I'd swear the air's alive with thought
as scientists of all nationalities   in complete silence
commune with their computers

study warming oceans   reef conservation
all human activities that affect
those delicate bridges between land and sea

the navigation suite hums with excitement
as illusion turns a perfectly stable room
into the seasick-making bridge

of whichever ocean-going vessel you choose
to practise on   as the world's ports rise
out of the atmosphere of mist and fog and rain to greet you

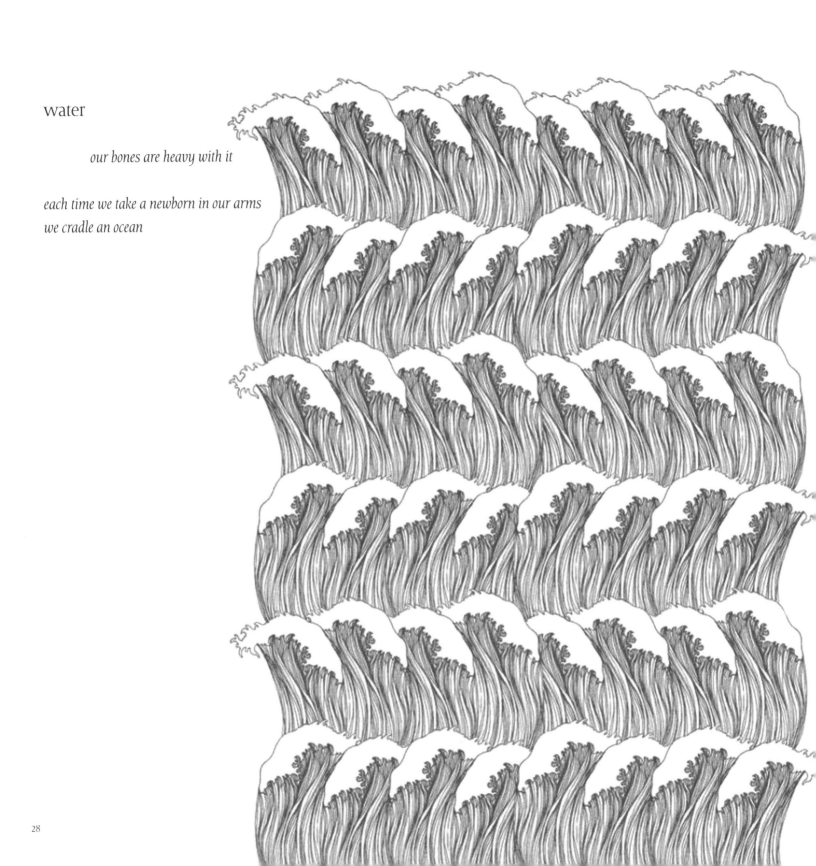

water

our bones are heavy with it

each time we take a newborn in our arms
we cradle an ocean

canal whale

stepping away from reality for one long reflective moment
this 68 foot narrowboat
whose huge length I'm looking over now
becomes a blue whale
a teenager   or at least a young one
sleek and confident as it glides to the lock gates
waits   enters
sinks slowly under an invisible blanket
as it would sink down under the sea
until the top wall of the lock is far above us
and I now sitting in its belly
admiring its carefully formed structures
wonder whether
if I step towards the bow
I'll find myself gazing through baleen curtains
into the open mouth of the ocean
as the gates open
and a rush of krill pours in

tsunami

everyone's running as if from a lifelong friend
who's suddenly picked up a gun
pointed it at us   the friend who only yesterday
watched us jumping back and forth
over shifting lines between sea and sand
watched as we played in the shallows
while inquisitive fish nibbled our ankles

only yesterday   we swam out over the reef
looked down at its secret gardens
where cherubs and angels mingled
with gobies and parrotfish   gaudy beings
from another world   flicking their tails
as they went about their business   changed course
without warning   where are they now?
can they survive his hard new face   the noise
as he slams himself ashore?

he can flatten small houses with one surge only
says my mother   two will take out the road
the third tear trees from their roots
but it's the fourth that kills
tosses boats ashore like outgrown toys

we're powerless as the ants
running up and down trees all day
travelling the unsafe corridors they've built
which can be punctured with one finger

and like ants we're running
from the friend who's become our enemy

when I first crossed the Atlantic by myself

anxious   wondering
if everything in my new life would be metal
(even the saltwater bath was made of it)
I hung over the side each day
watching the sea   sometimes dull sea blue
but more often iron grey   and wearing
a sullen expression   as if it mocked
the shuddering decks
the pistons thundering backwards and forwards
in deep canyons under the waterline

meals were in the canteen
(there were only 20 passengers)
I watched the waiter
balance a tin tray on one upturned hand
as if he wished he were on a more important ship
not sliding across the floor of a rough banana boat

each day I sat on a metal stool at the bar
asking for orange juice
till I drank the ship dry

each night I counted waves
clanking against the hull beside my head
while the minute hand of my new watch
crept round its small globe face
marking off another of the 14 days
on my makeshift calendar

I trembled each time my sleeping arm
crashed against thin steel plating
which was all that held out the sea

bulk mailing

someone's been sticking postage stamps on beaches
celebrating the wonderment of seabirds
pinning them out   like mad philatelists

glueing them down with the bounty from ships
that have flushed out their tanks

we marvel
at long drawn-out necks   feet in paddling position
eyes dimmed to a last sleep

all sent out in random mailings   the way people do

early morning swim
for Philip

tomorrow I'm going to take an early morning swim
while the light is fresh and the smell of the open ocean
creeps into the estuary with its twice a day promise
of staying forever   because the sea and the rivers
have the kind of marriage that promises everything
in the sanctity of the church or solemnity of the registry office
or even a toes-in-the-sand setting of a Caribbean beach ceremony

the tide will be in tomorrow   they'll be interweaving with each other
declaring their similarities and shared interests
their love of fish   openness to strangers and outsiders
the sea will be loving the land and overwhelming it with kisses
and declarations of going on for ever
but rivers know promises are seldom kept
there's too much foreign in each of them
their offspring will be the children of brackish water
the half and half life of mid-tide before the earth
takes back its distillations of mud and rain

like me waiting for tomorrow ...

you ask what's special about water . . .
for Chris

. . . why everyone gazes out to sea
as if something extraordinary's
about to unfold   and I explain
that when you reach the height of land
look down on the other side
unless there's the shimmer of lake or pond
or a river making its journey home
you see a place asleep   and if this view
opens out to the sea   framed by cliffs
sand   or rocky beach   you'll be standing
at the edge of the world

Pole of Inaccessibility
85° 47' N, 176° 9' E

There are four North Poles   but this is the true one
unmarked unvisited   on its bed of floating ice

not fixed as the Geographic Pole is   holding
like an Olympian charioteer   the reins of longitude together

not wandering   like its Magnetic brother considering travel options
and when it will arrive in Russia

not a time nomad like the Geomagnetic Pole
counting in centillions   planning its move South

(the Pole of Inaccessibility sighs like an octogenarian whale
when Geomagnetic's referred to as "True North")

no

under its air-blanket of Northern Lights
the Pole of Inaccessibility   a Rapunzel ice-maiden

lies in a Shangri-La of frozen Arctic Ocean
waiting for explorers who never come

> *although they may send messages*
> *lately   a Coca-Cola can*

moving house

her young son   sewn into his rough fur hides
looks out of the window laughing
as his house on its long skis jerks forward over the ice
pulled by reindeer   uneasily shaking their forest of horns

this family lives on the ice   is part of the ice
part of its morning and evening breath
its memories of leaf patterns
its love of slapping its hands together
as they follow seals walruses
whales cruising ocean hollow-ways
marking their paths with great funnels of water

we are all voyagers now
part of the moving skin of the world
woven into it like her son in his reindeer hides
learning why one part of the ice is not the same as another

listen!   her face shined by the northern lights
the woman is lulling her son to sleep
throwing her voice high in the heart-stopped cold
as she sings of arctic terns turning away from the dark
skimming ley lines of the upper air
on their annual journey to the other pole   and back

la mer

*the dream is gasping and moving through water   smooth and rare as the
vellum you're working on   where words glow like polished amber   and
syllables drop into the mind   like the gold leaf surround of each page
 and the woman who is this dream   is still as the hinged moment of the
day   that sits between memory and imagination*

*and she calls you into herself in the morning   when she's calm as new
spring flowers   bathing you in hope and orchids   in pictures of
reapers   gathering their skirts   as they harvest new season wheat*

*and she calls you into herself in the centre of your life   as her winds
 draw fire off the mountain   and two-headed monsters stretch long necks
into all four corners of the the universe*

*and she calls you into herself in the evening   when the sun is setting
 and her surfaces are sleek as the fur of a young otter*

*and now she calls you into herself in the moonlight   and this time she
wants to keep you   because   not only this great sea   but also the night
has transformed small waves into dreams so special   they can only be
found in the pages of the book you're working on   where words glow
like polished amber   and each syllable drops into the mind   like a
pearl dissolved in wine   which will be poured into a goblet of such
price   the world is still waiting for someone worthy to drink it*

surface tension

whatever fish-eaters tell us about the moon
and why it's moving further away

whatever meaning is left to us out of this tangle of love
this skein of wool that will never free itself from itself

whatever encounters there may be
on any busy street in any city   important or unimportant

when you touch the hand of a stranger   a friend
or even a lover you've known all your life

you'll be touching water that has been moving
and is still moving   round the full circumference of the world

Acknowledgments

These poems were completed during my residency with the Marine Institute, Plymouth University. An earlier version of "Blue Whale" has won a prize in the 2014 Kent & Sussex Competitiom, and "Dreaming the Ancestor" appears in the Extraordinary Forms anthology from Grey Hen Press. Big thanks are due to all the wonderful people I met and worked with during the residency, especially the VELMER group, with whom I shared my "hot-desk" space for many months.

I'm grateful to Neil Gaiman for giving me permission to use a quote from his book The Ocean at the End of the Lane.

I owe huge thanks to the Marine Institute for its warm and generous welcome, and to Tim Guy, who masterminded much of the project.

Caroline Carver would like to thank the following for their kind generosity for supporting this publication:

Professor David Coslett,
Interim Vice-Chancellor and Chief Executive, Plymouth University

Professor Martin Attrill,
Director of The Marine Institute, Plymouth University

Mr David Alder,
Chief Marketing Officer, Plymouth University

Mr Paul Wright,
past Senior Lecturer at the Plymouth University Business School

Paul is presently involved with various organisations including the Maritime Foundation, which among its activities recognises the value of the written word and media activity in raising public awareness on Britain's reliance on the sea. In recent years Plymouth University and the Maritime Foundation have collaborated in organising an annual conference, 'Britain and the Sea'.

Mr Andrew Eccleston,
past Senior Lecturer at the Plymouth University School of Navigation

Disadvantaged and disabled children in Plymouth are helped to get in touch with the sea by Horizons Plymouth Children's Sailing Charity.

A fleet of sailing dinghies and an army of volunteers give these children the opportunity to develop new skills and self-confidence through adventures out on the water. Andrew Eccleston is a Trustee of this charity and is developing links with Plymouth University.

Endnotes

p. 24 counting the infinite
the Secchi Disk was invented in the 19th Century by the Pope's Astronomer, Father Pietro Angelo Secchi, to measure the quantities of plankton in seawater. Today it is also a Citizen Science project, used to collect data by lowering a white disk into the sea until it is no longer visible, then sending the results to a satellite via an App devised by Dr. Richard Kirby.

p. 23 ocean silk roads
the CPR (Continuous Plankton Recorder) is a drum towed behind many merchant ships worldwide. It works by collecting plankton on a moving band of silk.
The project is managed and run by the Sir Alister Hardy Foundation for Ocean Science (SAHFOS), based in the Marine Biology Lab in Plymouth, and its research is used by an international network of scientific institutes and environmental organisations.

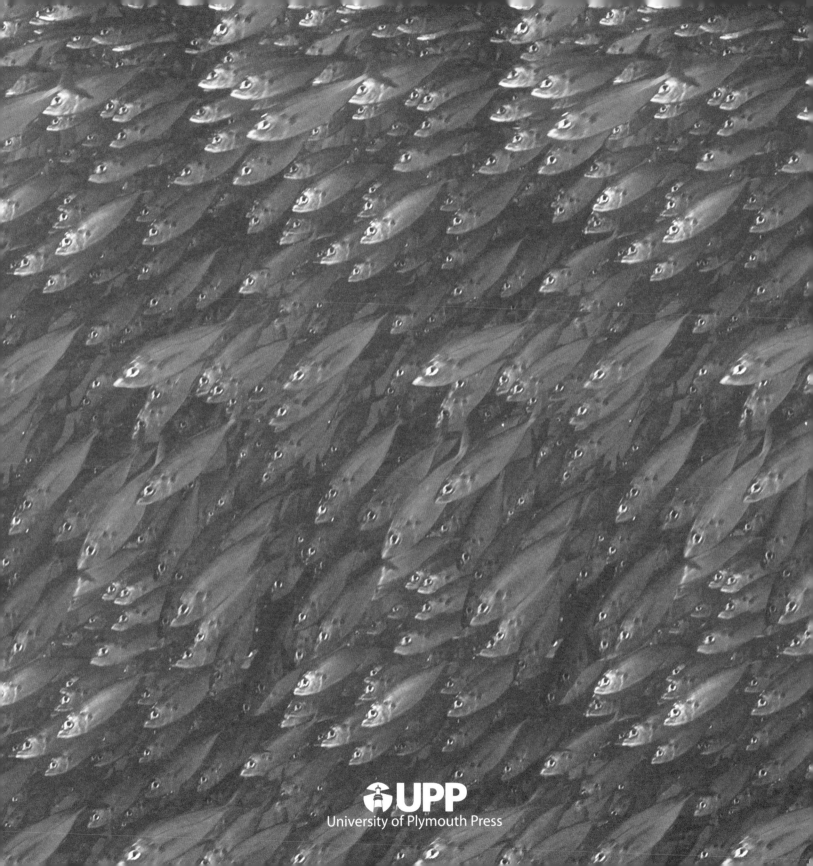